IN GRANDMOTHER'S
FOOTSTEPS

In Grandmother's Footsteps

A treasury of household hints from the past which save time and money today

ELIZABETH BEAUMONT

with a Foreword by
Jilly Cooper

THE BODLEY HEAD
LONDON   SYDNEY
TORONTO

Drawings by Eric Stemp

British Library Cataloguing
in Publication Data
Beaumont, Elizabeth
In grandmother's footsteps.
1. Home economics
I. Title
640   TX145
ISBN 0-370-30325-3

Printed in Great Britain for
The Bodley Head Ltd
9 Bow Street, London W2CE 7AL
by Redwood Burn Ltd
Trowbridge & Esher
Set in Monotype Ehrhardt
by Gloucester Typesetting Co. Ltd
First published 1980

CONTENTS

Foreword by Jilly Cooper, 7

1. Beauty Care and Cosmetics, 13

2. Your Health, 19

3. Kitchen and Cookery, 29

4. Household Cleaning, 45

5. Removing Stains, 55

6. Clothes and Materials, 69

7. Tasks about the House, 77

8. Flowers and Plants, 87

9. Animals and Vermin, 95

10. This and That, 103

   Index, 107

FOREWORD

Where cooking and housekeeping were concerned, I didn't have any grandmothers' footsteps to follow in. My paternal grandmother once ventured into the kitchen to talk to the cook, and was so appalled by the sight of a wet dishcloth lying on the sink, that she fled, never to return. From then on, instructions to the servants were only issued from the drawing-room sofa.

My maternal grandmother was a brilliant cook (my father claims that when he first visited the house he was almost more seduced by the delectable smell of rabbit stew floating out of the kitchen than by the beauty of my mother and her two sisters). But she cooked instinctively by pinches, a pinch of this here, a pinch of that there, so none of her wonderful recipes alas were passed down to future generations.

But if neither of my grandmothers taught me anything about running a house or cooking during my childhood, it seemed they were always around, grumbling, chiding, cherishing, advising, providing roots and a link with the past.

One of the saddest things about the present day is that the generations seem to spend less and less time together. Mothers go out to work, children go to nursery school at three. The moment they leave school or university, children move away from home, get a flat, and start forging a career of their own. There is no longer any time for mothers and daughters to keep house together before the daughter gets married, and for the wisdom of generations to be passed down, as it were, almost by osmosis. Even sadder, grandmothers are far less likely to be living with or near their families. When Granny is too old to look after herself, she is usually shunted into a home.

With so many marriages breaking up too, children go to live with one parent, and are often completely cut off from the opposite set of grandparents. Granny is therefore less and less often around to impart her pearls of wisdom.

This is perhaps one reason why I find *In Grandmother's Footsteps* such a charming and reassuring book. For, in no small way, it replaces some of those links with the past we seem to have lost. And what a wealth of information it provides. There are tips on cooking, housework, gardening, beauty care, looking after children and pets and on removing practically anything from everything. How I wish I had had the book to hand several years ago when my daughter wrote all over my neighbour's new and priceless pale green wallpaper with shocking pink lipstick.

At a time too when money is getting tighter, *In Grandmother's Footsteps* tells you a great deal about saving the pennies. This Granny knows all about thrift and re-cycling. Did you know, for example, that cigarette and cigar ash, cold tea, tea bags, bacon rind, even the juice of sauerkraut can all be put to good use? Granny also knew how to make everything from brooms to buttonholes last longer. Nothing need be wasted, bread can be made unstale, lettuce unwilted, even the dew is utilised to help with the washing-up.

Granny is good too on pets—getting rid of cat and dog fleas—even providing advice on how to catch a recalcitrant canary. My own cats particularly appreciated her tip on how to get rid of cockroaches by putting down herrings. They are even thinking of bussing in parties of cockroaches to the house, in the hope we might use such a deterrent.

In Grandmother's Footsteps, with all its tips on time-saving, must be required reading for the working girl, the busy mother, and the young bride, who suddenly finds she has to cook, go out to work, keep a house shining brightly and a husband happy at the same time. But it will also be invaluable to men. One of the phenomena of the last decade has been the emergence of the male cook sometimes through choice, more often through necessity. Here he will learn the most simple yet often unknown things: how to boil a cracked egg without losing the white, how to fry sausages without bursting them, how to skin tomatoes, and perhaps most important of all, how to tell when meat is cooked.

Granny can help with his courting too. How many romantic candle-lit dinners have been ruined by the smell of cauliflower or sprouts drifting out from the kitchen, fighting with the after-shave. Or what is the point of slaving over a delicious prawn provençal for your beloved, if afterwards when you try to stroke her hair, your hands reek most un-erotically of garlic? Granny's tips will remedy all this. Being a wily old bird, she also knows how to cure next morning's hangovers and bags under the eyes.

My own grandmother had a beautiful rose-petal complexion to the day she died, and claimed that this was due to the fact that her mother had taught her to wash her face in water distilled from elder flowers. Today when cosmetics only go on to the market after being tested by experiments involving appalling cruelty to animals, the back-to-nature beauty methods to be found in this book become particularly attractive. Granny shows that you can moisturise your skin, prevent a shiny nose, brighten up your eyes, lengthen your eyelashes, improve the condition of your hair, and keep a suntan going—without the need of chemicals. Nature can do it all.

Perhaps I recommend *In Grandmother's Footsteps* so warmly because it seems to have the right values. The old do matter. They have so much to offer us. And I hope if readers are as enchanted by this book and find it as useful as I have, they may seek out their grandmothers and other old people, gain invaluable advice from them, and in doing so make them feel needed.

For as my daughter pointed out the other day:

'A granny is only a double-decker mummy.'

Jilly Cooper

I
Beauty Care
&
Cosmetics

I

Beauty Care and Cosmetics

Get rid of *bad breath* by chewing coffee beans. If, however, you are suffering from indigestion chew cumin seeds daily instead.

A refreshing addition to your *bathwater* can be made with orange or satsuma peel. Let the peel soak in a bowl of water for two days and then filter the water through a linen cloth. Throw the peel away and add the water to your bath.

Chapped elbows and knees can be treated with the peel left over after you have squeezed a lemon. Place the peel over the chapped area and leave it for a short time.

A clean *comb* is important in keeping the scalp and hair healthy. Clean your combs with an old toothbrush dipped in ammonia and then rinse them in a weak solution of soda crystals.

Moisturising *cream* can be expensive. Save money and achieve much the same results by applying slices of raw potato to your face. Mayonnaise is also effective.

Erase bags under your *eyes* by soaking two pieces of cotton wool in lukewarm camomile tea or rosewater and leaving the resulting pads over the eyes for fifteen minutes. Then rinse your eyes and the skin around them gently with lukewarm water.

Tired *eyes* respond happily to a compress of used cold tea bags.

For long beautiful *eyelashes* brush them every night before going to bed with a toothbrush dipped in odourless castor oil.

The *face masks* our grandmothers made from natural ingredients were often gentler to the skin than more modern concoctions, less expensive and extremely effective. And they are still so today.

For *dry skin* make a mask from a raw egg yolk mixed with a teaspoonful of almond oil. Stir well and spread over your thoroughly cleansed face. Leave for twenty minutes and then rinse off with lukewarm water.

For *oily skin* use white of egg. This will tighten the skin and close any large pores. Whip several drops of lemon juice into the white of egg and apply to your clean face. Leave about twenty minutes and then rinse off.

Several *face masks* can be made from fruit:

The minced pulp of an avocado makes an excellent treatment for older, dry skin.

A mashed banana is very beneficial to a dry sensitive skin.

Mashed strawberries will make the skin soft and pure.

Fruit masks should be spread evenly, left on the face for ten minutes and then rinsed off with lukewarm water.

Bathe perspiring *feet* in a solution of alum powder and water. Repeat the treatment as necessary.

Remove brown nicotine stains from your *fingers* by rubbing them with lemon juice. The stains will disappear gradually. For very persistent stains add a small amount of hydrogen peroxide to the lemon juice.

Keep dirt or other materials from getting under your *finger-nails* by scratching them deeply into a cake of soft soap before performing grimy chores.

Bleach *freckles* with the regular application of lemon juice.

For glossy, healthy *hair* rinse it in beer after washing. Allow the beer to soak into the hair for several minutes and then rinse thoroughly with water.

Another way to have glossy *hair* is to rinse it with rose-mary water. Add four tablespoonsful of rosemary to two pints of boiling water, leave to cool and then filter. Rinse your hair with the resulting water.

For soft *hair*, rinse it with vinegar after washing. This will also keep it from getting greasy.

Treat *oily hair* by washing it with hot camomile tea.

Mayonnaise makes an excellent *hair conditioner*.

Grey hair will stand a good chance of regaining its natural colour if you wash it regularly with vinegar and water—one part vinegar to two parts water. This treatment will also be helpful in preventing your hair from turning grey although it cannot, of course, stop the process altogether.

For soft *hands* massage them daily with a cream made of equal parts of glycerine, lemon juice and natural honey.

Washing your *dirty hands* with coffee grounds will clean them thoroughly and also make them soft.

Treat *chapped hands* with a mixture made with two tea-spoons of almond oil, one teaspoon of honey and an egg yolk. Cover your hands with this concoction, put on a pair of cotton gloves and leave for one hour. Then remove the gloves and wash your hands with water and vinegar.

Another treatment for *chapped hands* is to massage them

with an oily cream and then rub a few drops of vinegar into them. The vinegar will contract the skin and heighten the protective effect of the cream.

A shiny *nose* should be rubbed occasionally with a slice of bad raw potato. Leave to dry after each treatment!

To improve the condition of your *scalp* and hair cut a medium-sized onion and rub it across the scalp several times. Then wash your hair in the usual way. This will also encourage the hair to grow.

If you find your *skin* becomes dry after a bath try adding the water in which spinach has been cooked to your bathwater. The same result can be obtained by making and using an extract of melon pips. Boil melon pips in water, allow to cool and then strain.

Treat an oily *skin* by adding a pinch of borax to the bathwater.

Get a quicker *suntan* by applying wine vinegar to your skin. But remember to let it dry before going into the sun or it could cause disfiguring brown stains. Perfume or toilet water will also cause a brown stain and should not be applied before going into the sun.

Before the invention of toothpaste people brushed their *teeth* with salt. Its abrasive quality is especially useful in removing tartar.

2
Your Health

2

Your Health

If you suffer from lack of *appetite* eat a lump or a spoonful of sugar with a few drops of lavender oil on it just before a meal.

Deal with a *bee sting* by removing the sting from the wound with a pair of tweezers. Then apply a piece of cotton wool soaked in ammonia and the pain should soon ease. In the case of a wasp sting there is nothing to remove. Just apply the ammonia.

Treat high *blood-pressure* by drinking tea made of four tea-spoons of dried shepherd's purse. Put the herb into a pot and add boiling water, leave it to draw for ten minutes and then strain. Two cups of this tea should be drunk daily, one in the morning and one in the evening.

Low *blood-pressure* can be treated by eating lots of hazel-nuts and berries, especially raspberries.

A nasty *bump* on the head should be rubbed with butter. This will make the skin flexible and enable it to yield to the swelling, which should lessen the pain.

A *burn* that is not too serious should be covered with the white of an egg, which should then be allowed to dry. Having done this there will be no need to bandage the burn as the egg white will protect it from dirt and infection. It will also ease the pain and help it to heal.

When you have a *cold* try sniffing a little ground camphor into your nostrils. It will disinfect the mucous membrane, ease the pain and relieve your head.

Drinking sweetened milk in which figs have been boiled or chewing on a piece of root ginger will also help to cure a *cold*.

Perspiring can also help. 'It will drive away the devil,' one grandmother used to say. Induce perspiration by drinking vast quantities of lime blossom tea.

Relieve *constipation* by eating dandelion leaves every day.

If you are troubled with *corns*, bind a small piece of onion over them. This is a sovereign remedy. Another received treatment is the daily application of a stoned grape. Bind the grape to the corn with a piece of linen or sticky plaster and replace every morning with a fresh one. After two or three days the corn can usually be removed.

To make your own *cough medicine* put a few slices of onion, some brown sugar and a little water into a pan. Leave to simmer for a few minutes and then drink.

Another home-made *cough medicine* requires three ounces of natural honey, one and half ounces of rum, one egg yolk and a tablespoon of olive oil or salad oil. Mix all the ingredients together and take a spoonful regularly.

Water in which potatoes have been cooked can also act as a *cough medicine*, provided it has not been salted. Drink it very slowly while it is still warm.

If you dab minor *cuts* with a piece of alum it will stop the bleeding and help to heal the wound.

There are a number of grandmotherly cures for *diarrhoea*. Try eating dried bilberries, or eat dry rusks and drink cocoa. The water in which rice has been boiled may also be drunk. Peppermint tea, also recommended, might be more comforting.

Avoid blistered *feet* by wearing shoes with leather soles and undarned socks. If you are planning a long walk or a walking holiday it is advisable to harden your feet beforehand. Rub them daily with camphorated spirits for several weeks. Or treat them daily with formalin powder.

A *fever* can be reduced by placing slices of lemon on the radial veins (the veins on the inside of your wrist). Renew the lemon slices regularly until the fever abates.

A *fever* may also be cured by drinking strong coffee with a teaspoon of lemon juice added. Sweetened grape juice or apple juice may also be beneficial.

Soothe *haemorrhoids* by applying a tea extracted from tormentil (a kind of cinquefoil) or from stinging nettles. It is also advisable to wash haemorrhoids daily with cold water.

Get rid of a *hangover* by drinking a cup of strong, sweet coffee containing the juice of half a lemon. It tastes terrible but it will put you right.

A *headache* can be helped by firmly rubbing up and down the gully at the back of the neck. Do this a few times.

Get rid of *headlice* by washing the hair and scalp thoroughly with hot vinegar.

People with weak *hearts* should drink a decoction made from the white felt-like partitions found in fresh walnuts.

Remedy *hoarseness* by slowly eating fried sweet potatoes.

If you are troubled with *indigestion* eat plenty of onions. Occasionally eating raw cabbage will also help.

An old-fashioned treatment for *influenza* was to add a cupful of hot water (not boiling) to three teaspoons of dried elder blossom. The brew was left to draw for a few minutes, then strained and drunk.

Cures for *insomnia* are legion. Try the old trick of placing a cold wet cloth over your eyes while lying in bed. Or repeatedly inhale deeply with your eyes open and then exhale with your eyes closed. This will make your eyelids feel heavy and encourage you to sleep.

Still awake? A slice of onion on a piece of hot toast may be the answer. Or drink dill and camomile tea.

Stop an *itch* by rubbing it with orange or lemon peel.

If you are stung by a *jellyfish* make a mixture of equal parts vinegar and water. Dip a piece of gauze into this and bandage the gauze over the sting. Keep wet with the vinegar and water until the redness and swelling disappear.

Treat painful *kidney stones* by drinking tea made from young birch leaves. Two cups of this tea will require only one third of an ounce of leaves.

Avoid having to taste unpleasant *medicine* by sucking an ice cube beforehand. The ice will deaden your tastebuds. This ruse is especially handy when you have to dose an ill but determined child.

Counteract *nausea* by eating a piece of dry bread toasted until it has begun to burn.

Nervous people should eat an egg whipped in milk for breakfast.

Nettle rash is extremely painful but should not be scratched. Rub it instead with dock leaves, which can usually be found growing close to nettles.

It is wrong to make people hold their heads back when they have a *nose bleed*. It is better to make the patient sit on a chair, with the head bent forward a bit, and to press the bleeding nostril for some ten minutes. If the bleeding has not stopped by then call a doctor.

Our grandmothers dealt with *nose bleeds* in a number of other ways. One method was for the victim to sniff lemon juice mixed with vinegar through the afflicted nostril. Shutting the mouth, breathing in deeply through the nose and then exhaling through the mouth was also said to help. A more colourful treatment was for a person bleeding through the right nostril to put the forefinger of the left hand into the bleeding orifice and hold the right hand up in the air for three minutes. After this the bleeding often stopped! And vice versa, of course!

Many a grandmother treated her *rheumatism* by drinking tea extracted from stinging nettles. One old lady of my acquaintance, who was not a grandmother but who easily qualified on grounds of age, insisted that walking barelegged through stinging nettles was also excellent for treating rheumatism. I often saw her doing it.

Herring with garlic is, inexplicably, a good remedy for *seasickness*. Dry bread soaked in a little vinegar will also help, as will dry biscuits. People who know that they may get seasick should remain lying down as much as possible.

Sleepwalking can be prevented by placing a large wet cloth on the floor by the side of the somnambulist's bed. As soon as his bare feet touch the wet cloth he will wake up.

Sore throats and swollen tonsils can be treated in many ways. Gargling with salt is a common remedy. Sage tea is also effective, and a more exotic treatment that can give immediate relief is to drink cucumber juice sweetened with natural honey. This should be drunk very slowly.

Soothe *sunburn* by placing slices of fresh cucumber over the afflicted areas. Yoghurt will also lessen the pain. Or mix a pinch of sodium bicarbonate into half a cup of milk and smooth this gently over the burn.

Sunstroke is extremely dangerous and a doctor should be sent for immediately. A sunstroke victim can be recognised by a flaming, scarlet face, a pulse quicker than normal (more than seventy beats per minute) and heavy perspiration. The victim is also likely to faint. Take him out of the sun into a shady, cool place (for example, inside a house) and fan him until the doctor arrives.

Prevent *sunstroke* by keeping the head and the back of the neck covered when it is very hot and the sun is shining fiercely. It is especially important to protect young children and elderly people from fierce sun.

A good remedy for *sweating* hands is to wash them with cologne several times. Washing them in a decoction of oak bark or in camphorated spirits will also be effective.

Prevent hands and feet from *sweating* by washing them regularly in water with a little alum powder dissolved into it.

The mercury in a clinical *thermometer* can be shaken down quite easily if you first allow it to cool.

Rub ingrowing *toenails* regularly with soft soap for about five weeks. After this the nail should grow straight again.

If you cannot get to the dentist immediately *toothache* can be treated with a strong decoction of cloves. Do not drink it but use it as a mouthwash. A piece of cotton wool or a cotton bud soaked in oil of cloves pressed against the aching tooth will also ease the pain temporarily.

Travel sickness can be prevented or eased with many types of tablets available at the chemist's but travelling grannies also had a few tricks. Eat some solid dry food such as biscuits before travelling. Make sure there is good ventilation in the vehicle and do not read if you find this bothers you. Children who suffer from travel sickness may be helped by wearing dark glasses.

Warts can be removed by regularly saturating them with onion juice. Rubbing them with the velvety inside of a broad bean pod is also said to be effective.

3
Kitchen
&
Cookery

3
Kitchen and
Cookery

Shelling *almonds* can be a patience-cracking chore. Try putting them in a pan of cold water, bring it quickly to the boil, and then drain the almonds and rinse them in cold water. After this they should be easy to shell.

Peeled *apples* will keep their colour if you sprinkle them with lemon juice. This trick is especially useful when making an open apple tart or any other dish where the apples will be exposed to the air for a long time.

Avoid lumpy *batter* by first adding a pinch of salt to the water called for in the recipe. Then add the flour.

Home-made *biscuits* often stick stubbornly to their baking trays. Outwit them by putting hot baking trays on to a damp cloth and leave them to cool. The biscuits should then come away easily.
  Biscuits will remain crisp if you put an ordinary sugar lump in the biscuit tin. Check occasionally to make sure that a small child has not taken the sugar along with a biscuit.

To make *braising steak* more tender smear both sides of the meat with a thin coating of mustard before cooking. This will also improve the taste.

When you are baking *bread* the dough will rise faster if you crush a fifty milligramme tablet of vitamin C and add this to the warm water in which you dissolve the yeast.

Your home *bread*-making will be more successful if all the ingredients and utensils you plan to use are at room temperature before you begin.

Cutting hot *bread* will be much easier if you first plunge the blade of the breadknife into boiling water for a few seconds. Wipe off any moisture left on the blade before using it.

Bread will keep longer if it is kept in an earthenware crock. Wash the lid of the crock once a month with cold water.

Revitalise stale *bread* by wrapping it in a damp linen cloth (a clean tea towel will do nicely) and placing it in a warm oven for a quarter of an hour. Don't get the oven too hot or the cloth could catch fire.

Breadcrumbs can be made quite easily without the help of modern gadgets. Bake slices of bread in the oven until they are quite dry and then crush them finely with a rolling-pin. This is a good way of using up stale bread.

Before the invention of refrigerators our grandmothers kept *butter* fresh by placing it in a stone bowl filled with salt water. Provided the bowl was kept in a cool place the butter would remain fresh for a considerable time.

Today, *butter* that has become too soft will probably get popped back into the refrigerator. But it can also be hardened quickly by placing it, still wrapped, under the cold tap for a few minutes.

Keep the smell of *cabbage* from spreading through the house by putting a small piece of lemon in the cooking water.

Cabbage will be easier to digest if a little cumin is added to the cooking water.

If the top of a *cake* is becoming too dark before its cooking time is over, quickly open the oven door and place a piece of greaseproof paper over the top.

To determine whether or not a *cake* is completely cooked, push a clean dry skewer into its centre. If the skewer comes out clean the cake is cooked. If there is any trace of dough sticking to the skewer put the cake back into the oven for a few more minutes and then repeat the test.

To loosen a *cake* from its tin use the same trick that was suggested for biscuits. Place the cake tin straight from the oven on to a damp cloth and allow to cool. Then turn it out.

To keep *cake* fresh put it in a tin which contains either a layer of brown sugar or a small piece of peeled apple.

Avoid the unappetising sight of grubs in cooked *cauli-flower* by winkling them out beforehand. Cut back the stalk as far as possible, place the cauliflower upside-down in a large bowl of cold water laced with a handful of salt, and soak for ten to fifteen minutes.

To prevent the smell of *cauliflower* from lingering put an old crust of bread in the cooking pan under the vegetable. This ruse will also work with Brussels sprouts.

Cauliflower will become beautifully white if you add a little milk to the cooking water.

Keep *cheese* from drying out by wrapping it in a moist linen cloth. Or wrap it in greaseproof paper and then in a second wrapping of aluminium foil. Greaseproof paper alone will not be effective. Store in a refrigerator if possible.

If *cheese* has not been properly wrapped and is already

31

dry, stand it in a bowl of milk for a while. Then remove it and allow to drain for several hours before using.

Cheese should not be eaten straight from the refrigerator as it will lose much of its flavour when it is cold. Bring it well up to room temperature before it is needed.

Intensify the luxury of real *coffee* by making it with mineral water rather than tap water.

Give *coffee* a novel taste by adding a pinch of cocoa and a pinch of salt to the grounds before pouring on the water.

Coffee can be reheated without any loss of fragrance or taste by warming it in a double boiler. Put the cold coffee into a small saucepan and place this into another, slightly larger saucepan which has been filled with water. Stand the pans on the cooker and bring the water to the boil. Once the coffee has heated through it will be as good as freshly-made.

In the days when *coffee* was hard to come by, some of our grandmothers made a substitute from wheat grain. This was thoroughly washed and then heated in the oven until it was a nutty brown colour. Once cooled it could be ground and used to make coffee in the normal way.

Prevent general *cooking smells* from lingering while you are working in the kitchen by filling a pan with water and adding a dash of vinegar. Bring to the boil and allow to steam freely.

Whipped *cream* can be made lighter by adding a little white of egg. The cream will go further, too, and optimistic fatties can pretend that it has slightly fewer calories.

If *cream* refuses to thicken when you are whipping it, try adding a few drops of lemon juice.

If your *currants*, or indeed any dried fruit, sink maddeningly to the bottom of cakes and bread, try washing the fruit, drying it thoroughly and then shaking it through a little flour before using it in the recipe.

Prevent skin from forming on cooling *custard* by sprinkling a little sugar over the surface.

Before handling *dough* rub a little salad oil into your hands. This should keep it from sticking.

To prevent *dough* from sticking stubbornly to a rolling-pin, cool the rolling-pin first in the refrigerator. If you do a great deal of baking store your rolling-pin in the refrigerator at all times.

To tell whether an *egg* is fresh dissolve two tablespoons of salt into one litre (two pints) of cold water. Place the egg in question in the water and draw the following conclusions about it from its behaviour:

FRESH: The egg sinks to the bottom immediately.

REASONABLY FRESH: The egg rests halfway between the surface of the water and the bottom.

BAD: The egg floats on the surface of the water. Do not use it.

Eggshells are porous and a certain amount of liquid will evaporate each day, resulting in a lighter and lighter egg. Fresh eggs should feel heavy and 'well filled'.

Eggs will not slip from your fingers if you dip your fingertips in water before picking them up.

Separate the white of an *egg* from its yolk by breaking the egg carefully into a clean funnel. Shake the funnel gently over a bowl and the white of the egg will pass through the bottom of the funnel, leaving the yolk at the top.

Keep an *egg yolk* fresh by placing it in a cup and covering it with cold water.

Prevent *eggs* from cracking during boiling by adding a dash of lemon juice or vinegar to the water. Or a small hole can be made at the rounded end of the egg, where the air pocket is located. The old-fashioned method of using a pin or a darning needle for this still works, of course, although the modern pricking gadgets are probably easier and safer to use.

Although an *egg* that is cracked or is doubtful in any way should be shunned, if, while handling it, you have cracked an egg which you know is fresh it can still be boiled. Wrap it in a moist piece of paper, taking care that the egg is completely covered. Then boil it in its paper wrapping, but cook for one minute longer than usual.

To keep the yolk from crumbling when slicing a hard-boiled *egg*, wet the knife before making each cut.

To quicken the process when whisking *white of egg* add a few drops of lemon juice to it, or a pinch of salt or sugar.

Fried *eggs* will taste much nicer and cook much faster if you pour a little melted butter over them while they are cooking.

Prevent *fat* from spitting by adding a little salt to the frying pan.

Should the fat in your frying pan catch *fire*, turn off the gas or electricity immediately and cover the pan with a tight-fitting lid, a baking tin or any other nonflammable object which will exclude air from the pan. Do not attempt to remove the burning pan from the cooker. If the fire continues to burn, throw salt, sand or bicarbonate of soda on to it, *but never water*, which may make fat fires spread, or flour, which may explode. If in any doubt or danger at all dial 999.

When frying *fish* add a teaspoonful of lemon juice to the fat. This will improve the taste of the fish and make the pan easier to clean.

A damp cloth hung over a gas cooker will absorb most of the smell of frying *fish*.

To remove the smell of *fish* from your hands wash them in beer.

The lingering smell of *fish* in the larder can be eradicated with milk. Fill a jug with boiling milk and stand it in the larder on a central shelf. Close the door and leave for at least an hour.

If you are fond of *fritters*, try beating a few pieces of grated apple in with the batter to give them a fresh, unusual taste.

Adding beer to *fritter* batter will give them extra lightness.

Prevent your hands from picking up the smell of *garlic* by wetting them first.

For families who insist on *gravy* to pour over their potatoes and vegetables even when they are willing to go without meat, try this early ersatz recipe: melt enough margarine in a frying pan to cover the bottom, grate a medium-sized onion and add it to the margarine when it begins to colour. Fry until the onion becomes transparent, stirring occasionally. Then add a peeled, mashed tomato (or, more simply, some tomato puree), a few dashes of Maggi or Worcester sauce, and stock. Season to taste.

Add a pinch of sugar to the butter in which you fry meat and you will be rewarded with a rich brown *gravy*.

Braising steak will develop a thick *gravy* if you add a piece of rye bread to the pan.

For a very thick *gravy* try adding oatmeal rather than flour.

Don't throw away *honey* which has dried. Put the honey jar in a saucepan filled with warm water and heat very gently until the honey liquefies. Do not allow the water to come to the boil as this may crack the jar.

A cut *lemon* can be kept for up to a fortnight by placing it cut side down on a saucer covered in a layer of granulated sugar. Keep in a cool place.

Revive a limp *lettuce* by leaving it for thirty minutes in cold water to which a tablespoon of lemon juice has been added.

Macaroni and spaghetti will not stick together if you add a knob of butter or a small amount of cooking oil to the cooking water.

Washing *meat* can make it tough. Wipe it instead with kitchen towels and perhaps some salt. The high temperatures used to fry, grill or roast meat will kill all bacteria.

Judging whether or not a joint of *meat* is cooked is a simple matter of colour-coding and requires a gadget no more sophisticated than a thin knitting needle or a skewer. Pierce the thickest part of the joint (or chicken or other fowl) with the knitting needle and the juice which runs from the meat will tell you all you need to know:

Red juice means the meat is still rare.
Pink juice means the meat is also pink.
White (or clear) juice announces that the meat is thoroughly cooked.

Wetting your hands before making *meatballs* will keep the meat from clinging to your fingers.

Milk will not burn if you stir some sugar into it.

If milk does burn it is often difficult to get the saucepan clean again. Try filling the saucepan with water, put in a raw onion and boil. The crust of burnt milk should come away easily.

You can prevent *milk* from boiling over by smearing a little butter around the rim of the saucepan. The milk will not rise above the butter-line.

Milk will not turn sour if you add a pinch of bicarbonate of soda to it.

To remove *mince* easily from its greaseproof paper simply hold it under cold running water for a few seconds.

Dried-up *mustard* can be salvaged by stirring a little vinegar and a pinch of sugar into it. To keep mustard from drying out mix in a little salt.

Oats can take the place of nuts in many recipes. Fry the oats in a little margarine or butter until they are brown and crisp.

Keep a cut *onion* fresh by placing it cut part down on a saucer covered with kitchen salt.

In the days before tearproof mascara, our grandmothers knew several good ways of preventing their eyes from watering and stinging while they were peeling *onions*. Try placing the onion in a basin and covering it with boiling water. Once the water has cooled the onion can be skinned without tears. Or simply hold the onion under water while peeling it. And your eyes will not sting if you hold a sip of water in your mouth while you are peeling. But don't swallow until you've finished.

You can get rid of the smell of *onions* on your breath by drinking a glass of milk.

If your *oranges* come wrapped in tissue paper, do not throw the paper away. The fruit will last much longer if left in their wrappings.

Oranges will peel easily if you stand them in boiling water for ten minutes and then let them cool in cold water.

Oranges will yield more juice if, before squeezing, they are rolled back and forth on a table under the pressure of your hand.

As with fritters, the batter for your *pancakes* will be lighter if you add a dash of beer.

Try replacing some of your *pancake* flour with custard powder for a lovely golden pancake with a delicious smell.

To keep the *pastry* of a fruit tart from becoming dismally soggy spread the pastry with white of egg, allow to dry and only then add the fruit.

Pâté will cut cleanly, without sticking to the knife, if you first wet the blade with cold water.

Give an added flavour to green *peas* by putting a piece of lettuce in the cooking water. Or try a sprig of mint. Remove before serving.

Sprinkle freshly-cut *pineapple* with lemon juice to keep it from discolouring and to improve the flavour.

Prevent peeled *potatoes* from discolouring by putting them in a basin of salted water. Leave for about five minutes and they can be transferred to fresh water with no chance of their changing colour.

To keep peeled *potatoes* fresh overnight put a slice of dry bread at the bottom of the saucepan of water in which you are keeping them.

To ensure that all your *potatoes* are cooked simultaneously use ones that are more or less the same size. If necessary take a knife to them and cut them into equal pieces.

To give boiled *potatoes* a more delicate taste, boil them only a short time and then drain. Return them to the cooker in a pan of fresh, cold water, add the required amount of salt and cook as usual.

To cook *potatoes* more quickly add the salt five minutes before you would normally expect them to be done, or add a knob of margarine or butter to the water.

To make your *potatoes* look white add a little milk to the cooking water.

If an unattended pan of boiling *potatoes* should burn, don't throw the lot away. Remove the burned potatoes and put the rest back on the cooker in a clean pan with fresh water and the required amount of salt. Pretend nothing happened; all trace of the taste of burned potato will have disappeared.

When frying *potatoes* never put a lid on the pan or they will lose their crispness and become soft and soggy.

Fried *potato chips* will turn a beautiful golden brown if you dust them with flour before cooking.

To make sure your boiled *rice* is white and dry, just add a little lemon juice to the saucepan. Alternatively, drain off the water, place a slice of stale bread over the rice and replace the lid. The dry bread will absorb any moisture that is left.

Keep *salad oil* clear by adding a teaspoonful of salt to it.

Salt will remain dry and free-running if you put ten grains of rice in the salt-cellar.

Sausages often burst during cooking. Some people are quite partial to exploded bangers but, if you are not, put the sausages in hot water for a few seconds and then cover with flour before cooking them. Or soak them first in cold milk.

To make sure that your vermicelli *soup* is elegantly clear, cook the vermicelli separately and add it to the soup at the last moment.

You can remove grease from *soup* by placing a double layer of kitchen paper on the top of the soup. Press it gently onto the surface and the paper will absorb most of the grease.

For a quick *soup*, put a tablespoonful of tomato ketchup with two teaspoonsful of margarine into a cup and top up with boiling water. Add salt and pepper to taste.

Putting too much salt into *soup* need not be a disaster. Peel a potato and cut it into slices, add to the soup and simmer for about fifteen minutes. The pieces of potato will absorb the surplus salt.

Wash *strawberries* before removing the stalks. They will become soft and watery if you wash them after the stalks have been removed.

Peeling *tomatoes* can be difficult as well as time-consuming. Put the tomatoes in a basin and cover them with boiling water for no more than thirty seconds. They will then be very easy to peel. The same trick can also be used with peaches.

Walnuts will crack with little effort if you first bake them for a few minutes in a hot oven.

4
Household Cleaning

4
Household Cleaning

Aluminium pots and pans will not discolour if a spoonful of vinegar is added to the water when you are boiling eggs or puddings. A discoloured aluminium pan will come clean again if rhubarb, apple peel or a spoonful of cream of tartar are boiled in it.

Salvage a badly burned *aluminium* pan by boiling an onion or rhubarb leaves in it until the burned bits float to the top. But remember that rhubarb leaves are highly poisonous and should be thrown away and the pan rinsed thoroughly after this treatment.

An old-fashioned trick for cleaning a *baking tray* is to leave the tray dirty-side-down on the lawn overnight. By the following morning the dew will have softened any hardened matter stuck to the tray and it will come clean easily.

Baking trays and tins will stay free of rust if they are covered with lard when new and heated thoroughly in a hot oven.

Bottles, carafes and decanters can be made spotless with potato peelings or shredded newspapers. Fill the dirty container with water, some salt, and the paper or peelings. Shake well, empty and rinse with fresh water. Finely broken eggshell can be used in the same way (without the salt) and will be easier to work with when cleaning glass vessels with narrow necks. If the container is especially dirty, shake, leave the mixture to soak overnight, shake well again and then rinse.

To remove strong smells from *bottles* or other glass containers you want to use again, such as medicine, spirit or spice bottles, half fill with cold water and add a tablespoonful of dry mustard. Shake well and leave to stand overnight. Then shake again and rinse thoroughly.

Clean your *breadboard* occasionally by rubbing it with a piece of lemon dipped in salt. Rinse and leave to dry, preferably in the sun. This will bleach it beautifully white again.

Bronze can be cleaned by sponging it with water in which you have cooked haricot beans without salt. Polish afterwards with a chamois leather.

Spruce up a pair of *brushes* by sprinkling flour on both of them and rubbing the bristles backwards and forwards against each other.

A dirty *candle* can be cleaned by wiping it with a cloth moistened with petrol. Don't, of course, do this when the candle is lit. Leave the petrol to dry and the candle will be as new.

Candle wax can be easily removed from a copper or silver candlestick by holding it in hot water. The wax will quickly soften and can be peeled off.

China coffee or tea pots often have a brown stain caused by tannin. Remove this by pouring a strong, hot soda solution into the pot. Leave it to stand for several hours or overnight. Then scrub clean and rinse thoroughly.

Brown stains on *china* coffee or tea cups can be removed by rubbing the stain with salt.

Chromium coffee and tea pots should never be cleaned with soda. Instead, any tannin stains should be rubbed with a cloth moistened with vinegar and dipped in salt. Rinse immediately in boiling water and wash well before using.

Chromium can be polished with a soft cloth moistened with ammonia. Polish afterwards with a duster. Or sprinkle with baking powder and polish with a dry cloth.

Remove rust from *chromium* with aluminium foil or silver paper. Wet the foil and rub it firmly over the rust until it disappears. Then polish with a soft cloth.

A *clothes brush* can be cleaned by placing a piece of white paper over the edge of a table and rubbing the brush over the edge. Move the paper slowly along so that the brush is always being rubbed on a clean piece of paper. Repeat until the paper remains clean.

Clear out an old-fashioned *coffee grinder* occasionally by putting a handful of rice through it.

Brighten *copper* with a paste made of equal amounts of flour, salt and vinegar. Rub the copper with the paste, then rinse and dry thoroughly. If the result is a bit disappointing, do it again, but more firmly.

Another excellent *copper* cleaner can be made by mixing soap, brandy and French chalk. Or, if you are fond of sauerkraut, wash your copper with sauerkraut liquor and then rub it with a cloth sprinkled with cigarette or cigar ash.

You can make *copper* glow by rubbing it with a piece of cut lemon before polishing it. Or rub with lemon and then pour boiling water over it, dry and polish with a soft cloth.

Polish small, intricate *copper* objects by soaking them in sour milk for a few hours. Then rinse with water and rub dry.

Dusting will be easier if you prepare the duster by washing it and adding a few drops of glycerine to the last change of rinse water. Dust will then be attracted to the treated cloth.

Enamel pans sometimes develop a crust on the inside which is caused by hot water. Remove this by boiling out the pan with sugar-water.

To make drinking *glasses* shine brightly, put them into water to which you have added some baking powder. Afterwards just leave them to dry.

Iron objects can be protected against rust for years on end by putting them in a solution of soda for about fifteen minutes. Then remove the objects from the soda solution and leave them to dry.

Iron pans will become as bright as silver if you rub them with hot salt.

Remove rust from *iron pans* by rubbing them firmly with the fatty side of a piece of bacon rind.

To remove fur from a *kettle* fill the kettle with water and add vinegar and a handful of salt. Bring to the boil, turn off the heat and allow to cool. The fur will become loose. Then empty the kettle, shake out the fur and rinse the kettle several times with fresh water.

Kettle fur can also be removed with potato peelings. Half fill the kettle with potato peel, top up with water and boil for about an hour. Then empty it, shake out the fur and rinse thoroughly.

Prevent *kettle* fur forming by putting several clean glass marbles into the kettle and leaving them there.

Rusty *knives* can be brightened by rubbing the blade with dry mustard sprinkled on a damp cloth. Or push the blade into earth. This treatment will also remove the smell of fish and onions from knives.

Prevent *metal* objects from becoming dull by placing an ordinary piece of blackboard chalk in the drawer or cupboard with the objects.

Mica can be cleaned with vinegar or methylated spirits.

Triumph over a very dirty, greasy *oven* by turning it to 'hot' for about twenty minutes. Then turn off the heat and place a saucer of ammonia on the top shelf and a large pan filled with boiling water in the bottom of the oven. Close the oven door and leave it overnight. The following morning open the door and leave the oven to air for some time. After this it should be easy to clean with ordinary soap and water.

Avoid grease building up in your *oven* by wiping it while it is still warm after every use with old newspaper.

Clean a frying *pan* by holding the underside of the pan under the hot running tap immediately after use. When the hissing has stopped quickly turn the pan over and clean the inside with a brush, keeping the pan under the hot running water all the time.

Yellowed *piano keys* can be whitened by carefully wiping each key with a solution of equal parts water and methylated spirits applied to a damp cloth. Lemon juice, eau-de-cologne and alcohol are also effective. Be careful not to let liquid spill between the keys.

Plaster ornaments often pose a dilemma. Make a paste with either a spoonful of starch mixed with a little warm water or potato flour dampened in the same way. Spread the mixture on the plaster ornament, covering all surfaces. Leave to dry in an airy place and the mixture will loosen and fall away, taking any dirt with it.

Remove *refrigerator smells* by thorough washing with vinegar and water after defrosting. Or crush several charcoal tablets and put them on a saucer in the refrigerator. After a short time the smell will disappear.

Polish *silver* more easily by soaking it first in potato water.

To make tarnished *silver* shine again crumple up a piece of aluminium foil, put it into a bowl filled with water and add a handful of salt. Leave the silver in this water for a few hours. Then just rinse and dry it.

Another economical method our grandmothers used to polish *silver* was to put the silver object into an aluminium pan containing a gallon of water, a tablespoonful of salt and one of baking powder. After leaving silver in this solution for some time it can be removed, rinsed and dried well and will shine beautifully.

Silver can also be polished with a soft cloth dipped in cigar ash.

Blackened *silver spoons* can be brightened by rubbing them with a little salt.

Refresh a *sponge* by soaking it in buttermilk for some time. Then wash it and rinse in water and soda.

Rust spots on *steel* can be removed by rubbing them with cork or with petrol. Stubborn spots will disappear if you rub them with a cut potato coated with emery powder.

To clean a *thermos flask* and remove the sediment of coffee or tea, crush an egg shell and put the pieces into the flask. Add some hot water and replace the stopper. Shake well for a few minutes, then empty the flask and rinse several times.

A *thermos flask* will not develop a musty smell if two lumps of sugar are kept in it when stored.

When using a *tin opener* occasionally put a piece of kitchen paper between the cog wheels and the tin to clean it.

Remove *verdigris* easily by washing it away with ammonia.

Wallpaper can be wiped clean by rubbing it with a dry natural sponge sprinkled with some bran. Or rub with a piece of bread that is at least three days old.

You can make a special dough for cleaning *wallpaper* by mixing two parts of flour with one part turpentine substitute in a basin. Add one part warm water and knead the mixture into a thick dough. Then wipe your wallpaper with long firm strokes, always exposing a clean part of the dough to the paper.

Before *washing up* add a piece of lemon peel to the water. This will soften the water and make dishes shine beautifully.

For clean, shining *windows* make a mixture of one part vinegar to two parts water. Put this in a soda syphon and spray it over your windows. Then polish the panes and they will shine brightly.

Windows can also be washed effectively with water in which you have soaked potato peelings. Or polish the panes with a flannel cloth on which you have sprinkled some flour.

Bird droppings on *window* panes can be removed in a trice by rubbing the spot with a cloth soaked in vinegar.

If you are plagued by greasy *windows* remove the grease by rubbing the glass with a cut lemon.

5
Removing Stains

5

Removing Stains

General tips for removing stains

A stain can be removed more quickly and more easily when it is still fresh. So do not give it a chance to dry.

When you are going to remove a stain from a garment or any other piece of material try out the stain remover first on a spot which is not visible when wearing or using it.

Remove as much as you can of the cause of the stain before you actually start cleaning.

Always rub in the direction of the thread.

Be extremely careful when you are using white spirit, methylated spirits or alcohol. With all these there is a great risk of fire.

Our grandmothers were especially fond of a stain-removing solvent called trichloroethylene, which is abbreviated throughout this section to 'tri'. Although trichloroethylene may still be obtained from chemists under various proprietary labels, its popularity has been supplanted by carbon tetrachloride and all the advanced quick-and-easy cleaners and solvents now on the market. These products may be used in the place of 'tri' when it is mentioned in this chapter, but remember to use makers' instructions carefully. Do not smoke when using these volatile products, keep them away from heat and flame and use in an airy room or out-of-doors.

Textile stains

It is often said that *beer* does not stain. But this is not true. Fortunately the stain is easy to remove. Just wash it out with lukewarm water.

Stains caused by *beeswax* can best be treated by soaking them with turpentine. After this the material should be rinsed thoroughly.

Beetroot can cause nasty stains. These should be rinsed out first with water and then with pure alcohol.

Bird droppings should be first left to dry and then brushed off.

The stains caused by *blackberries* are difficult to remove if not treated immediately. Stretch the stained part of the fabric over a basin and pour boiling water over it. If the stain cannot be dealt with immediately cover it with salt. Rub borax into a dried stain, pour on boiling water and soak for ten minutes. Rinse thoroughly and then wash.

Fresh *bloodstains* can best be removed by rinsing them with cold or cold salt water and then washing in the ordinary way. Dried *bloodstains* should be soaked for one to twelve hours in water to which a spoonful of ammonia has been added. Then wash normally.

A piece of brown paper (or ordinary toilet paper) can be very useful if there is a *butter* stain on textile. Wipe the spot clean with paper, taking care that you do not spread the butter further. Then soak the spot with white spirit or tri.

To remove *candle wax* from clothes or any other textile, first scrape off the surplus, then cover the spot with brown paper and put a hot iron over it. The wax will melt and be absorbed by the paper. If necessary, repeat this until the stain has completely lifted.

Candle wax on linen can be removed by rubbing the spot with methylated spirits, having first scraped off the surplus.

Cherry stains will disappear if you first wash the material in soapsuds and then soak it in milk for some twelve hours. Alternatively, rub the spot with alcohol and then wash the material thoroughly.

If you accidentally spill *chlorine* on any material, forget any idea you may have of removing the stain. There is just no way of doing it.

Chocolate can usually be washed away with hot water and soap suds. Scrape off as much as possible before washing. Sponging with soapy water containing some ammonia may also be effective, or sponge, rub with dry borax, leave for half an hour and then wash.

To remove *cocoa* stains first wash the material and then dip the stain in sweet milk until the milk has turned sour. Or firmly sponge the stain with glycerine and then wash it in lukewarm water.

Sponge away *coffee* stains with a mixture of glycerine and egg yolk. Before using this method try to wash the stain out with ordinary warm soapy water.

Stains caused by *cream* should be treated by sponging them with lukewarm water. After this any remnants can be removed with tri.

Face *cream* can be removed from clothes with white spirit or tri. After this the material should be washed thoroughly.

Currant stains can be removed if you soak them with diluted ammonia. After this you can wash the stain out quite easily.

White of *egg* can best be washed out with cold water. But the stain caused by yolk should be treated with lukewarm water and liquid soap.

Glycerine can be removed from textile fairly easily. Sponging it with lukewarm water should do the trick.

Grapejuice stains should be soaked carefully with methylated spirits, after which the spot should be washed.

A persistent *grass* stain can be removed by soaking it with alcohol.

If you have spilt some *gravy*, absorb it with some kitchen paper, then sponge the spot with some white spirit or tri. After this, the material should be washed thoroughly.

Grease stains should be dusted with potato flour. Leave it for a while to soak up the grease, then brush off the flour and the grease will come off too.

Ice cream stains should be washed out with lukewarm water. If necessary treat them with white spirit or tri.

Ink stains can be divided into different categories:
   Ordinary ink can best be blotted with a tissue. Then soak the stained spot with vinegar, buttermilk or milk. Keep

applying until the stain disappears, then wash thoroughly.

It is also possible to remove an *ordinary ink* stain with hair lacquer. Spray lacquer over the stain, leave it to soak in for some fifteen minutes, then rinse thoroughly.

Ballpoint stains should be soaked with methylated spirits or acetone. White textiles can be soaked in buttermilk or vinegar. Repeat the soaking if the stain is stubborn.

Stamp-pad ink is best removed with white spirit or tri. If, after this, some ink is still left in the fabric, try rubbing it with alcohol.

Indian ink can be washed out with plain or soapy water, but only when the stain is fresh. Old stains are difficult to remove, but try rubbing them with alcohol. Wash thoroughly after this.

Remove fresh *iodine* stains with warm soapy water containing a little ammonia. An old stain may be treated with wool bleach, but make sure the fabric is suitable.

Do away with *jam* stains by first scraping off as much as possible, then sponging the spot with lukewarm water. Persistent stains may be treated with water containing a little borax or ammonia. Or rub with lemon juice and wash again thoroughly.

If you spill *lemon juice* over your clothes, rinse it out as soon as possible with lukewarm water. Lemon juice very quickly affects colours.

To remove *lipstick* from clothes rub the spot with alcohol or tri. The material should then be washed thoroughly. Lipstick stains can also be treated with glycerine. Remember to wash thoroughly.

A stain caused by *liqueur* can be removed very simply. Wash the material with lukewarm water and, if necessary, sponge the stain with alcohol. Rinse afterwards.

Liquorice stains can be washed out with a solution of ammonia. The material must be thoroughly rinsed afterwards.

Spilt *mayonnaise* can leave a nasty stain on your clothes. To treat this, first scrape off as much as possible and then sponge the stain with tri or white spirit. If the stain has not lifted completely, it should be treated with a solution of ammonia. This too should be rinsed thoroughly afterwards.

Lukewarm soap-suds are usually all you need to lift *milk* stains. Should this not work, try using a little tri or white spirit.

Mud stains usually look worse than they really are. The best way to treat them is to let the mud dry, then brush it off with a stiff brush. This will usually do the trick. But if not, the remaining stains will disappear if you wash the material.

Stains caused by *nail polish* can usually be removed with a little acetone. Be careful, though. Acetone is harmful to some synthetic materials.

It is best to remove *nicotine* stains with methylated spirits. Take care that you wash the material thoroughly.

An *oil* stain should be soaked with white spirit or tri. Then the material should be washed well.

Paint stains can be removed with turpentine or white spirit. Old stains should be smeared with soft soap and left to soak for twenty-four hours. Then use the above method.

Stains caused by spilt *perfume* can be removed by soaking them with alcohol. It goes without saying that after this you must wash the material.

Perspiration stains should be treated with a solution of ammonia.

If you get *plaster* on your clothes, immediately rinse them out with a solution of vinegar. If the plaster has become hard, pulverize it first and then treat it as above.

Spilled *porridge* should first be removed with a spoon or with absorbent paper. The stain can then be removed by washing the material in soapy water.

Stains caused by *pus* wash out quite easily.

Resin stains can best be removed with turpentine. To treat an old, persistent stain dissolve the resin with some turpentine, then place a tissue underneath the stained area and press with a hot iron. Repeat if necessary.

To remove *rust* stains, cover them with a little lemon juice. Put a moist cloth over the stains and press with a hot iron. Another method from our grandmothers' day is to hold the stains over boiling tea, soak them with a little lemon juice for a very short time, and then wash the material thoroughly.

Scorch marks can be removed in a number of ingenious ways. Remove light scorch marks immediately by soaking the fabric in milk. Rub white fabrics with lemon juice and leave them in the sun to dry. Scorched linen can be rubbed with an onion and then soaked in cold water. Or try rubbing a scorched fabric with a linen cloth soaked in hot water containing chloride of lime (not too much!). Scorch marks

61

caused by a hot iron should be sprinkled with a weak solution of borax. Then iron the material until it becomes quite dry.

Lift *shoe polish* stains with turpentine. Wash the material afterwards.

To lift *soot* stains first cover them with talcum powder. Then brush the powder together with the soot from the material. Treat the remnant of the stain with white spirit or tri. After this the material must be washed.

An excellent general old-fashioned *stain remover* is the water in which haricot beans have been cooked without salt. With the use of this even persistent stains will disappear.

Strawberry stains can generally be removed by washing them out with lukewarm water. If this proves unsuccessful, try the borax method suggested for blackberry stains. Cotton and linen fabrics may also respond to being rubbed with lemon juice.

Suntan lotion will cause greasy stains, which can be lifted with white spirit or tri. As usual, it is necessary to wash the material thoroughly after using either of these liquids.

Tar stains can be removed with turpentine. Another way to lift them is to smear the tar stains with unsalted butter. After a while scrape off the surplus butter carefully. Then clean the spot with benzine and after this with methylated spirits. Wash the material immediately.

Sponge *tea* stains with lukewarm water. However, if the stain has dried, use a little methylated spirits. The use of lemon juice may have the same result. But wash the material thoroughly afterwards.

Stains can be caused by red or white *wine*. They require different methods to remove them.

White wine can be washed out with lukewarm water. If it is a persistent stain it should be treated with alcohol after washing.

Red wine causes stains which require immediate action. Cover the stain with salt and leave it until the wine has been absorbed. Wash the material as soon as possible.

Wood stains can usually be removed with pure turpentine. Moisten the stain with this and leave it to soak for some time. Then rinse with water. The stain can also be soaked with diluted ammonia and then washed out. For wool it is better to use turpentine than ammonia.

Yoghurt stains should first be allowed to dry, then thoroughly brushed. After this treat the spot with tri.

Stains on non-textiles

Stains on *copper* can be removed with a paste made of equal amounts of flour, salt and vinegar. Rinse the copper and dry it thoroughly.

Stains on *formica* are best treated by covering them with lemon juice (a piece of cut lemon with the pulp placed over the stain will also do). This should be left to dry and then the stain can be wiped off with a moist cloth.

Stained *marble* can be cleaned with a little copper polish on a soft cloth. You might also try cleaning it with a little bleach. It will be necessary to wash it with soap suds immediately after using the bleach.

Rust on *marble* can be removed by covering the stain with a mixture made of benzine and chalk. This should be covered with cellophane (or a plastic sheet) to prevent the benzine from evaporating too quickly. This treatment should be repeated every six hours until the stain has lifted.

Stains on *tin* can easily be removed by rubbing them with methylated spirits. Allow to dry and the stain will disappear. It will be necessary to repeat this if the stain is persistent.

Grease stains on *wallpaper* can be removed with a paste made of talcum powder and liquid soap. Cover the stain with this and leave to dry. Then brush it off and . . . the stain has disappeared completely!

A leaking water tap can cause brown stains in a bath or a *washbasin*. To remove the stains, pour a little buttermilk over them and leave it to soak in. The buttermilk can then be rinsed off, taking the brown stains with it. Lemon juice rubbed on this sort of stain will also be effective. A persistent drip will continue to create stains and further removal treatment will be required.

Stains on *wood* can be removed by smearing them with butter mixed with the ash of cigarettes or cigars. Leave the butter to soak into the wood. Then polish.

Ringmarks can be removed by rubbing them with the kernel of a walnut until the mark has disappeared. Leave the oil that has come from the nut to soak into the wood for a while. Then finish by polishing with a soft cloth.

Another way to remove marks on *wood* is to pour some

olive oil or salad oil into a saucer and add six drops of vinegar. Wind a cloth around the tip of your finger and mix the two liquids. Then with the moistened cloth rub the mark firmly. After a time you will find that the mark has disappeared.

A white stain in polished *wood* can be removed by holding a hot poker just above it. Generally, the white stain will disappear.

A stain in polished *wood* can also be treated as follows: put some cigar ash over the stain and add a few drops of water. Rub firmly with a piece of cork for some time. Then rub over the stain with a cloth which has been moistened with methylated spirits.

Candle wax stains on *wood* can be removed with an oil-soaked cloth.

6
Clothes
&
Materials

6

Clothes and
Materials

A crocheted *bedspread* can be handwashed. To dry it, spread it over a table while it is still wet and pin with drawing pins.

Waterproof leather *boots* by first cleaning them thoroughly, then covering them with thick soapsuds. Leave them to stand for some twelve hours before wiping.

If your *buttons* keep coming off, try sewing them on with very thin brass wire. Or sew the button back on with ordinary thread and then coat the thread with colourless nail polish.

In our grandmothers' day the procedure for cleaning greasy *coat collars* was rather elaborate. First the collar was covered with hot isinglass and left for six hours. Then it was smeared with hot soft soap and left for a further six hours. With a hard brush, dipped in brandy, the isinglass and soap were then brushed from the collar.

A simpler procedure for cleaning less dirty *collars* was to rub them with powdered magnesia or, on light-coloured collars, a piece of stale bread.

If you are going away for a visit and want to take *coat-hangers* it is advisable to take wooden ones. You can unscrew the hooks from the hangers so that they take up much less room in your luggage; put the hooks in a plastic bag.

Always fold your *clothes* into your suitcase in such a way that the folds are across the garments. When you unpack your clothes and hang them up the weight of them will soon pull out the creases.

An old *felt hat* can be made beautiful again if you wipe it with a cloth moistened with petrol. Do this out-of-doors and away from naked flames and cigarettes.

Flannel should not be washed in very hot water or it will become hard.

A *fur coat* can be cleaned by rubbing it with bran. Then gently shake and comb the coat. This process may have to be repeated several times.

To mend the fingertip of a *glove* put a glass marble into it.

To remove *hair* from clothing dampen your hand and wipe it firmly over the material. Or run a piece of sticky plaster or Sellotape over the garment.

When *ironing*, dampen your clothes with hot water rather than cold. This will dampen them more quickly and evenly.

To make your *ironing* smell fresh and sweet add a few drops of perfume or cologne to the dampening water.

If your *linen cupboard* is damp, put some cloves on a saucer and place it inside the cupboard. The dampness will quickly disappear.

To waterproof *linen*, first mix together five parts soap, five parts gelatine and seven parts alum, then make a solution from one part of this mixture and ten parts water. Immerse the linen in the solution, remove and allow to dry thoroughly. Repeat two or three times.

To *mothproof* your winter clothing while washing it simply add a dash of turpentine to the water. Or sprinkle your clothes with turpentine before putting them away for the summer. An orange spiked with a few cloves will help to keep moths out of a linen cupboard.

Patent leather shoes will keep their gloss if they are rubbed with a linen cloth soaked in sweetened milk. Do this regularly.

Patent leather can also be polished with an onion. Rub the leather with a raw onion, allow to dry and then polish with a woollen cloth.

Patent leather will not crack if it is rubbed from time to time with salad oil. Give the oil time to soak in before polishing.

Shampoo can be used as an effective general spot and stain remover for clothing. Put a little shampoo over the spot or stain and soak for twenty-four hours. Then wash the garment as usual.

Shiny patches on suits or other garments can be removed if you brush them with a solution of vinegar.

Shoes made of fine leather will remain soft and glossy if they are rubbed daily with raw white of egg. The small amount of white generally left behind in an eggshell will be sufficient.

Wet *shoes* should not be dried close to a stove or fire. Instead, stuff them with old newspaper and leave in an airy place. Allow them to dry completely and then polish.

If you must polish a pair of *shoes* when they are wet add a few drops of milk to the polish.

Your *shoes* will have extra shine if they are rubbed before polishing with a cut raw potato.

If your *shoe polish* has dried out mix a few drops of turpentine with it and the polish will soon be smooth again.

If you find you are out of *shoe polish* rub your shoes with the inside of a fresh banana skin. Let it dry and then polish with a woollen cloth.

If you are afraid of getting polish on your socks or feet when you are polishing your *shoes*, put your feet into paper or plastic bags and then put on your shoes. If the brush or cloth then goes above the shoe, the dirty bags can simply be thrown away.

To remove a grease stain from leather *shoes* smear a little rubber solution (of the kind used for mending tyres) over it. Allow the solution to dry, then pull it away and the stain will come with it.

If the ends of your *shoelaces* are frayed, twist the ends into points and dip them into a bottle of colourless nail polish. Allow to dry before using.

Silk ties can be cleaned with the juice from potatoes. Grate a few potatoes, squeeze them out in a towel and clean the ties with the juice you obtain.

Spectacles will not mist over if they are smeared with glycerine on both sides and polished with a chamois leather. Repeat the treatment from time to time.

Clean *suede* by wiping it with a cloth dampened with vinegar. Then scrub gently with a clean, hot brush. Use a toothbrush for small areas which need special attention.

Remove raindrops from *suede* by gently wiping it with a piece of fine emery paper.

To hang up a *sweater* to dry without having to put up with

the dreadful marks left by clothes-pegs pull an old pair of tights through the sleeves of the sweater and tie the feet of the tights to the clothes-line.

Trousers will dry more quickly if they are hung inside out so that the pockets and seams are exposed to the air.

A silk *umbrella* or parasol can be waterproofed by opening it and covering the fabric with a mixture of fifteen parts benzine to one part paraffin. Paint the solution over the top of the umbrella in straight lines, working from the centre to the edge. Use a soft brush.

Crushed *velvet* can be restored to its original beauty if you wrap a damp linen cloth around a hot iron and press the velvet very gently.

Remove grease stains from *velvet* by rubbing it with a flannel cloth moistened with turpentine.

Whiten your hand *washing* by putting some slices of fresh lemon tied up in a small cotton bag into the water.

Pre-shrink knitting *wool* before winding it by putting it in a pan or basin and pouring boiling water over it. Leave until the water becomes quite cold and then let it dry at room temperature.

A *zip fastener* that does not run smoothly can be eased by running a pencil lead over the teeth of the closed zip. Do this several times and the graphite will act as a lubricant.

Zip fasteners should be closed before a garment is washed to prevent it from being damaged or from catching on other clothing.

7
Tasks about the House

7

Tasks about the House

Warped *boards* can be straightened by placing them on a flat surface for twenty-four hours and covering them with a wet cloth.

Put away *brooms* with the bristles upwards or hang them with a piece of string through a hole at the tip of the handle. This will keep the bristles off the floor and make them last longer. New bristle brooms will also last longer if you put them in salt water overnight, then leave them to dry before using for the first time. Do not use this treatment with modern nylon or plastic varieties.

Soft bristle *brooms* can be made hard again by soaking them in water to which you have added a little ammonia.

Candles will burn longer and not drip if they are chilled in the refrigerator for twenty-four hours before they are lit. Or dip a whole candle (except the wick) into soapsuds and then put it in a candlestick to dry. This will also keep it from smoking.

Salt is also effective: soak *candles* in salted water for an hour before use and they will not drip. Sprinkle a small amount of salt on to the melted wax at the top of a burning candle and it will burn longer.

A *candle* will go out by itself if you place a rubber band

around it. As soon as the candle has burned down to the band the flame will go out.

You can make a *candle* fit almost any candlestick by putting the base of it into hot or boiling water for a short time. If a candle is too thin for the candlestick, fold a piece of aluminium foil into a long narrow strip and wrap this around the end of the candle until it is thick enough to fit tightly into the holder.

To clear a blocked *drain* pour a boiling hot solution of soda crystals into it. Take care that the boiling liquid goes directly into the drain as, with some enamel basins, it could cause cracks.

If a *drawer* sticks persistently and no other cause for obstruction can be found, try rubbing the runners with talcum powder, candle wax or plain household soap.

Clean a *file* quickly by holding it in steam for a short time.

An old *file* can be made usable again by rubbing it firmly with a piece of charcoal. This treatment will also remove rust.

To restore leather *furniture* simply rub it with whipped white of egg. It can also be polished with a mixture made from half a glass of milk and twenty drops of turpentine. With both methods take care to clean the leather thoroughly first so that you do not rub over any dirt or stains.

Heighten the gloss on polished *furniture* with a piece of cotton wool dipped in linseed oil or petroleum jelly.

Take the guesswork out of locating a *gas leak* by covering the suspected part of the gaspipe with soapsuds. If there is a leak it will blow bubbles.

Rubber *gloves* will last longer if you pull them inside out and stick a piece of sticking plaster on the inside of each fingertip. Or put a small piece of cotton wool inside each finger end.

If there is no *glue* in the house, paper can be securely stuck with lightly whipped white of egg. In the old days this was used for sealing envelopes and had an added advantage: it is impossible to steam open an envelope stuck with egg white.

Make an inexpensive *glue* by first washing the surface of the parts to be glued with soda water. Allow to dry thoroughly and then paint each surface with onion juice before sticking together.

To store a *hot-water bottle* for a long period, hang it upside down with the stopper removed until it is completely dry. Then shake some talcum powder into it and put it away, still with the stopper out. Tie the stopper with a piece of ribbon through the little hole at the bottom of the bottle.

Before filling a new rubber *hot-water bottle* for the first time pour into it a few drops of glycerine. This will make it more flexible and longer-lasting.

You can make the bottom of an *iron* smooth and bright again by scouring it with a mixture of vinegar and white sand.

Achieve the same effect by rubbing a candle stub against the bottom of the *iron* while it is still hot. After this treatment run the iron over a piece of blotting paper a few times before using it again.

Your *ladder* will not slip if you nail a small piece of rubber over the bottom of each leg.

To preserve *linoleum* clean it once a month and wipe it with a mixture of equal parts milk and water. Let this dry, rub with turpentine with a little wax dissolved in it, leave this to soak in for a minute and then polish the floor with a flannel cloth or a brush.

It is much easier to drive *nails* into soft wood than into hard. But nails can be driven into hard wood more easily if you first dip them into oil or stick them into a cake of soap.

If the point of a *nail* is blunted or cut off with a pair of pliers the nail will not split the wood.

A *nail* that has loosened in a wall can be made firm again by taking it out, wrapping some cotton wool tightly around it and dipping it into ready-made plaster. Drive the nail together with the cotton wool back into the wall and it will remain firm.

In addition to the usual methods for filling holes in walls made by *nails* or screws you can use toothpaste.

An *oil lamp* will give more light if you put a small piece of camphor about the size of a pea or a pinch of salt into the oil.

Tins of *paint* should be stored upside down.

To keep the smell of *paint* from spreading through the house, chop some onions and put them on a saucer in the middle of the room to be painted. Or add a fifth of an ounce of vanilla to each litre of paint.

Remove *paint* from glass by covering it with a thick layer of soft soap. Allow some time for the soap to soak in before washing it away.

To remove spilt *paint* from a cork wall dip a linen cloth in a little acetone and wipe the spot carefully.

Remove *paint* from your hands by covering it with a dab of mustard. Rub thoroughly and then wash away.

A new *paintbrush* will last much longer if you treat it in the following way: rub the bristles across your hand a few times to make any loose ones fall out. Then suspend the brush in a bowl of water for some twelve hours. This will make the wood expand and free the brush of any remaining loose hairs.

Or wash a new *paintbrush* with soap and water, vigorously massaging the bristles. Then rinse thoroughly with clean water, squeeze to remove as much water as possible and dry with brown paper. Dip the ends of the bristles into linseed oil and then leave for twelve hours. Before using it wipe the brush clean and put it into turpentine.

To enable you to put a *paintbrush* down while taking a break from your work, tap two little nails into the wood of the handle before you start, just below the metal. The brush can then be stood on the nails, keeping the bristles away from the floor.

To keep a *paintbrush* flexible overnight wrap it tightly in aluminium foil.

A *paintbrush* that has become hard can be restored if you let it simmer in vinegar for a few minutes. Then wash with soap and water, wipe the bristles with brown paper and allow to dry thoroughly.

You can also soften and clean a hard *paintbrush* by soaking it in a fifty per cent solution of carbolic acid.

Or stand a hard *paintbrush* in a jar of soft soap and leave it to soak for some time. This method will take a little longer than the others.

To make an unbreakable *rope* mix a small amount of alum

powder with some water and leave the rope to soak in the solution for twenty-four hours. Allow ample time to dry afterwards before use.

To keep the metal lid of a *salt-cellar* from rusting coat the inside with a thin layer of transparent lacquer or colourless nail polish. Leave this to dry and then prick out the holes.

To prevent a *saw* from rusting rub it from time to time with a greasy piece of bacon rind.

If you have difficulty in *sawing* a piece of wood rub a piece of soap across the teeth of the saw.

To fix a *screw* that keeps coming undone, remove the screw, put some steel wool into the hole and then replace the screw. Turn it tightly and it should stay firm.

To remove a rusty *screw* from wood place a hot poker on the head of the wedged screw for about five minutes. After this it will come out easily.

Make your *stair carpet* last much longer by putting old newspapers on the treads underneath the carpet.

There is less chance of a *vase* falling over if you fill it a third full with sand.

Rock-hard tubes or pots of *water-colours* can be made soft and usable again by adding a little water and glycerine. Tubes must be cut first and the contents put into old cups or other containers.

Windows will not become misted if you clean them with a mixture of one fluid ounce of glycerine to one pint of methylated spirits. Clean both inside and out. Repeat the treatment from time to time.

To prevent *windows* from frosting clean them with water to which you have added a handful of salt.

To prevent *wooden posts* from rotting in the ground cover the bases with a mixture of linseed oil and powdered charcoal.

8
Flowers
&
Plants

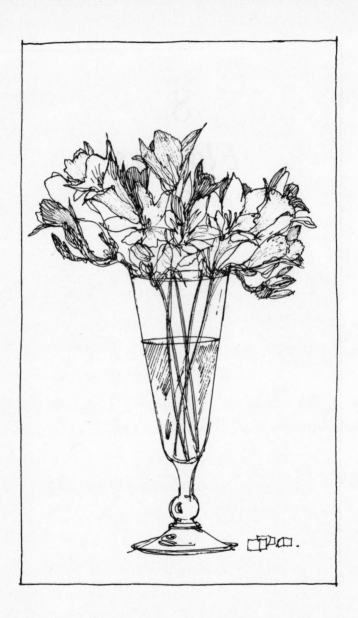

8

Flowers and Plants

Ants loathe *African marigolds* so plant some of these useful flowers in parts of the garden where you like to sit and especially where you are likely to eat outside.

The *African violet* requires a great deal of light but cannot tolerate direct sunlight. Put the plant under a lamp in the evening and this will encourage it to flower profusely.

Carnations should never be sprayed with water. To make them last a long time keep them in a cool place and add a dash of soda water and a pinch of sugar to their water.

Christmas trees will keep festive through the holidays if you put them in a two-to-one mixture of water and glycerine. Fir tree branches will also thrive in this solution, especially if the branch is cut at an angle.

Chrysanthemums tend to make the water in which they stand discolour and develop a strong rather funereal smell. Prevent this by adding a teaspoonful of bleach to the water.

    Chrysanthemum leaves will not droop and turn brown so quickly if a little sugar dissolved in warm water is added to their vase.

Before putting *daffodils* into a vase, cut the white end from the bottom of the stem and wipe away the white sticky substance that comes from it.

To keep *daffodils* longer only put an inch or two of water into their container at a time. Replenish as necessary.

Daffodils and tulips are not compatible and should not be arranged together in the same vase. The white liquid from the daffodils will quickly kill the tulips.

Our grandmothers had many methods of keeping *flowers* longer which can be equally effective today.

When *picking flowers* from your own garden do so very early in the morning when the leaves and stems are full of moisture. Cut them at an angle with a sharp knife and place them immediately in water.

A little salt or some sugar dissolved in the water, some pennies or a slice of lemon at the bottom of the vase, changing the water daily and snipping off a small portion of the end of each stem daily will all help to preserve them.

Wilted flowers can often be revived by dissolving an aspirin in their water.

Before putting *flowers* with woody stems into a vase split or smash the ends of their stems and plunge them into hot water for a short time.

Yellow *flowers* will generally keep longer than other colours.

Never put *flowers* near fruit. In particular pears, apples or bananas will have a destructive effect on the flowers.

Several kinds of *flowers* give off a sticky juice which is often called the 'blood' of the plant. Prevent cut flowers from 'bleeding' by holding the whole of each stem in hot water for a few minutes before arranging them in a vase.

A *flower* for a buttonhole will stay fresh if you singe the bottom of its stem.

Freesias especially are happier with a little sugar in their water.

Fighting grannies combated *greenfly* by spraying the invaded plants with soapsuds. Dusting the soil around the plant with cigar or cigarette ash was another ploy.

Make the *leaves* on houseplants glossy by cleaning them with a natural sponge soaked in a little milk.
Leaves on houseplants will not develop brown dis-colourations if they are sprayed with rain water rather than tap water.
When watering ferns, keep the *leaves* from turning brown by carefully lifting them out of the way of the watering can. Half an aspirin in the water will also keep fern leaves green.

Lilacs, like all woody-stemmed flowers, will last longer if their ends are crushed before they are put in a vase. Buy or cut lilacs which have already started to bloom or they will not open fully in the vase.

Lilies should have their stems cut at an angle and then be put in water right up to their necks. It is advisable to cut off their stamens, which are full of sticky pollen.

Make your rooms smell of *pine* by putting one teaspoon of turpentine into a bowl and pouring over it two pints (one litre) of boiling water. You will have to repeat this about three times a day to keep the fragrance strong. In Switzerland in the old days this method was used to relieve the suffering of consumptive patients.

Pollen can stain your clothing and furniture badly. Either the stamens can be removed from cut flowers, as recommended with lilies above, or consider spraying them with hair lacquer. Do your spraying carefully and from some distance away.

Poppies should have their ends singed before they are put in a vase.

When *potting plants* cut an old pair of tights into squares and put these at the bottom of each pot before filling with earth. The fabric will prevent the earth from falling through the pot and will also keep the pot clean.

When *re-potting plants* make sure to use a new pot of the correct size. A pot which is too large will encourage the soil to go sour because the roots will not reach it.

Stinging nettles can best be pulled by holding them at the base of the stem and running the hand up, and so flattening the nettles.

Sweet peas should not be cut when they are wet and when put into a vase should only be put in shallow water. Otherwise the water will climb up the hairy stems and discolour the flowers.

Before putting *tulips* into a vase wrap them in wet newspaper and put them, still wrapped, into two inches of water. Leave them for one hour and then unwrap them and arrange. This will keep them straight for much longer. A few pennies at the bottom of their vase will also keep them from drooping.

Never change the water in a vase of *tulips*. Just add to the existing water as required.

Water which has been boiled for tea or coffee, or in which you have boiled an egg, is best for plants because it is free of lime. So don't throw it away. Pour it into your watering can.

Water for houseplants should always be at room temperature.

A houseplant should not be allowed to stand in *water*. If you see water in a saucer or in the bottom of a cache-pot pour it away at once.

9
Animals
&
Vermin

9

Animals and Vermin

Ants out-of-doors can be discouraged by sprinkling the areas where you have seen them with lemon juice or by laying down pieces of cut lemon. They also dislike African marigolds (see the chapter on flowers).

Ants in the house call for a mixture of a pinch of yeast and a few tablespoons of treacle. Put this down everywhere they have been at work and they will have gone within ten days. They can also be warded off with small pieces of camphor or sage leaves.

Bees and wasps can be kept away by a small saucer filled with ammonia.

Pet *birds* are often troubled by lice. Get rid of the lice by hanging a small piece of oakum in the bird's cage. To prevent lice in the first place hang a piece of tobacco in the cage.

Bugs, like ants, will keep away if you put down sage leaves regularly.

If your *canary* has got out or been let out of its cage and you cannot catch it, wait until dusk. The bird will then remain stock still and you will be able to pick it up easily.

Fight off *cockroaches* by putting down a moist cloth where

they have been seen. Check the cloth every morning to see if it has attracted any cockroaches. Kill them immediately and replace the cloth with a fresh one.

If even the sight of a cockroach makes you cringe put down salted herrings. Cockroaches do not like the smell of these and will eventually go away.

Discourage *crickets* by leaving about the house pieces of white paper covered in a mixture of borax, flour and sugar. Stir these ingredients together thoroughly.

Ward off strange *dogs* by scattering flowers of sulphur on paths and lawns. Or grow the herb of grace in your garden.

A *dog* suffering from fits would once have been given raw eggs mixed with pepper and cinnamon.

Earthworms aerate the soil, but if you wish to discourage them scatter wood ash over the bed.

To get rid of *earwigs* fill a clay flowerpot with moist straw and place it upside-down on the spot where you have seen the earwigs. They will collect together in the straw and after twenty-four hours you can dump out the straw and burn it, earwigs and all.

Earwigs are fond of dahlias so shake the flowers well before putting them into a vase. Do this out-of-doors.

Fleas should be caught and then killed by holding them between the fingers under water. Wash down the drain and rinse with boiling water.

Cat fleas can be combed from the fur with a fine-toothed comb dipped frequently into lukewarm soap suds. Your cat will not get fleas if you put dried camomile flowers into its basket.

Dog fleas can be eradicated by occasionally washing your dog with water to which you have added a little creosote. Never, ever use this treatment on a cat. To discourage the fleas put some dry fern leaves under the dog's blanket.

If you are pestered by *flies* put a few drops of lavender oil on a couple of new bath sponges and put these on saucers in the room where you (or the flies) are.

Other old-fashioned tricks of chasing away *flies* include putting some laurel oil on a plate, hanging a piece of basil in the room or putting a piece of cut lemon on the window-sills.

Bluebottles have a particular aversion to burnt melon rind and will also stay away from meat that has been covered with slices of raw onion.

Make your own *fly poison* by mixing one part of finely ground black pepper with two parts of brown sugar and dissolve this in some milk. Put this brew down where flies will eat it and, as the song goes, they will surely die.

Rid your bedroom of *gnats* by passing a cup filled with petrol around the walls at night before you go to bed. The gnats, drugged by the vapour, will fall into the cup. Or put a piece of camphor on the bottom of a hot iron or a heated iron pan and walk with it through the room. Two other old gnat-chasing tricks are to leave the door and windows of your bedroom open (because gnats hate draughts) or to put a few drops of lavender oil on your pillow. This remedy is also thought to be soporific, so even if the gnats are not affected you may fall asleep and not notice them!

If your *guinea-pig* or *hamster* has young, try to avoid disturbing her for four or five days afterwards. If disturbed too often during this early period the new mother is likely to eat her young. After about five days she should have out-grown her cannibal inclinations.

Chase away *mice* by scattering fresh or dried mint leaves, cotton wool soaked in peppermint oil, cayenne pepper or sunflower seeds near the mousehole. The sunflower seeds will kill them.

Moles will move on to someone else's garden if you soak a cloth in petrol and put it in their run. The earth from a molehill makes a good fertiliser, incidentally.

Keep away *moths* by putting today's newspaper into the linen cupboard. Replace it every day with that day's paper. Moths find fresh printing ink so offensive that they'd rather go somewhere else to look for nourishment.

If you keep *pigeons* remember that they need a great deal of air. Make sure that their loft is well ventilated, especially in the summer.

Discourage *rabbits* from invading your garden by planting a few rows of onions or foxgloves around its perimeter.

Rout *rats* by blocking up the entrances to their holes with pieces of cloth soaked in engine grease. Or put down some chopped valerian where they have been seen. But remember that although valerian drives away rats, it attracts cats.

Get rid of *snails* by putting down wet newspaper. They will gather on the paper and can then be destroyed by sprinkling them with salt.

A *tick* can be dealt with by putting a little salad oil on it. This will smother it and it can be easily removed.

A *sheep tick* will first appear as a little wart, which will then turn purple and grow quickly within a few days. Get rid of it by putting tincture of iodine on it as soon as possible.

There is a very simple way to catch *woodlice*. Cut a potato and hollow out both halves, put them on the ground and the woodlice will soon nestle in the hollows. Do not kill them; put them on the compost heap where they will do a great deal of good breaking down the vegetation.

Woodworm in furniture can be destroyed with petrol or benzine. Dip some cotton wool into either and moisten the affected areas of wood. Better still, inject either liquid into the holes with a hypodermic syringe. Remember that this method is not suitable for polished wood as petrol or benzine will spoil the polish. And bear in mind that there is a fire risk with either petrol or benzine. Do not smoke while you are working and observe the other usual precautions.

Woodworm may also be destroyed by putting a fresh acorn on or next to the affected wood. Replace with a fresh acorn every day. Do this for a week and the woodworm will be destroyed.

Woodworm in cane furniture can be removed by submerging it in water for two days.

10
This
&
That

10
This and That

The *address* on a parcel will become indelible if you rub the stub of a candle over it firmly.

Make a *bed-warmer* that will never leak and will remain hot much longer than a hot-water bottle: fill a strong linen bag with fine white sand and heat it in the oven before putting it into the bed.

If your children enjoy *blowing bubbles* make them more colourful by adding a few drops of glycerine to the suds.

An ordinary paperclip can be used as a *bookmark*. Spare the binding of the book by placing the paperclip on the side of the book.

An excellent and practically invisible glue for *glass* can be made by melting some alum on an iron spoon.

A *glass* will not crack when you pour hot liquid into it if you place it first on a wet cloth.

Did you know that you can write on *glass* with a pointed piece of aluminium?

To make *invisible ink* mix one part of linseed oil to twenty parts of ammonia and one hundred parts of water. Write on paper with this mixture and as it dries it will become invisible. To bring the writing back place the paper in water. When the paper dries the writing will disappear once again.

Bleach is a good *ink* eradicator. Dip the end of a match into the bleach and carefully wipe away what you have written.

If a *parcel* is very fragile wrap it in soaking wet newspaper. Use lots of paper. When it has dried it will have formed a tough hard shell that will withstand a great deal of rough treatment.

A *piano*, and indeed all furniture, should not be placed within ten inches of the walls of a house less than one year old as the walls will still be damp.

Make a useful *pin cushion* that will also sharpen your pins by filling a small tough cloth bag with fine white sand. Make certain that the sand is bone dry by heating it in the oven. If it is at all damp the pins will rust.

A dented *ping-pong ball* can be put right by placing it in a bowl of hot water for a minute. The heat will expand the air in the ball and it will pop back into shape.

Sharpen *scissors* by cutting a piece of emery paper with them several times.

A *sewing-machine needle* can be sharpened by running it through a piece of emery paper.

Test suspect *silver* by soaking it in salted water. If the object is genuine silver nothing will happen. If it is fake it will turn violet.

A cake of *soap* will last longer and will be less mushy if you press a piece of aluminium foil against the side of the soap that rests on the basin.

Do not throw away remnants of toilet *soap*. Put them, together with a few drops of glycerine, into an old cup and place the cup in the steam from boiling water until the soap becomes soft. Leave it to cool and then knead into a ball. You can then press this into the form of a cake of soap between the palms of your hands.

If your *stamps* have stuck themselves together do not try tearing them apart. You could of course soak them but you will find it easier to place them under a tissue and run over them with a hot iron. This treatment will separate the stamps and also leave the glue on the back undamaged.

If you dislike the taste of the glue on the back of *stamps* lick the envelope instead.

To make the *string* around a parcel really tight wet it first. It will shrink as it dries.

Old metal *telephones* can be polished with a little copper polish on a soft cloth. This will make all scratches disappear.

Our grandfathers were also canny: they stored their *tobacco* in an airtight tin with a few potato peelings.

To get the last remnants of a product out of a *tube* dunk it first in a bowl of hot water.

INDEX

African marigolds, 87
African violets, 87
Almonds, shelling, 29
Aluminium pans, 45
Ants, 95
Appetite, lack of, 19
Apples, preserving colour, 29

Bad breath, 13
Baking trays, 45
Bathwater, 13
Batter, 29
Bedspread, crocheted,
    washing, 69
Bed-warmer, 103
Bee sting, 19
Beer stains, 56
Bees, 95
Beeswax, 56
Beetroot stains, 56
Bird droppings, 56
Biscuits, 29
Blackberry stains, 56
Blood-pressure, 19
Bloodstains, 56
Boards, warped, 77
Boots, waterproofing, 69
Bottles, 45-6
Bread, 29-30
Breadboard, 46
Breadcrumbs, 30
Bronze, 46
Brooms, 77
Brushes, 46
Bubbles, 103
Bugs, 95
Bump on the head, 19
Burns, 19

Butter, 30
    stains, 56-7
Buttons, 69

Cabbage, 30, 31
Cake, 31
Canary, 95
Candles, 46, 77-8
Candle wax, 46, 57
Carafes, 45-6
Carnations, 87
Cauliflower, 31
Chaps, 13, 15
Cheese, 31-2
Cherry stains, 57
China, 46-7
Chlorine, 57
Chocolate stains, 57
Christmas trees, 87
Chrysanthemums, 87
Clothes brush, 47
Clothes, packing, 70
Coat collars, greasy,
    cleaning, 69
Coathangers, packing, 69
Cockroaches, 95-6
Cocoa stains, 57
Coffee, 32
    grinder, 47
    stains, 57
Colds, 20
Combs, 13
Constipation, 20
Cooking smells, 32
Copper, 47-8
    stains on, 63
Corns, 20
Cough medicine, 20

Cream, 32
  moisturising, 13
  stains, 58
Crickets, 96
Currants, 33
  stains, 58
Custard, 33
Cuts, 20

Daffodils, 87–8
Decanters, 45–6
Diarrhoea, 21
Dogs, 96
Dough, 33
Drain, blocked, 78
Drawer, sticking, 78
Dusting, 48

Earthworms, 96
Earwigs, 96
Eggs, 33–4
  stains, 58
Enamel pans, 48
Eyelashes, 14
Eyes, bags under, 14
  tired, 14

Face cream stains, 58
Face masks, 14
Fat, cooking, 34
Feet, perspiring, 14
  avoiding blisters, 21
Felt hat, 70
Fever, 21
File, 78
Fingernails, 15
Fire, frying-pan, 34
Fish, 35
Flannel, 70
Fleas, 96–7

Flies, 97
Flowers, 88–9
Formica, stains on, 63
Freckles, 15
Freesias, 89
Fritters, 35
Frying pan, cleaning, 49
Fur coat, cleaning, 70
Furniture, 78

Garlic, 35
Gas leak, 78
Glass, 48, 103
Gloves, mending, 70
  rubber, 78–9
Glue, home-made, 79
Glycerine stains, 58
Gnats, 97
Grapejuice stains, 58
Grass stains, 58
Gravy, 35–6
  stains, 58
Grease stains, 58
Greenfly, 89
Guinea-pigs, 97–8

Haemorrhoids, 21
Hair, to remove from
  clothing, 70
Hair care, 15
Hamsters, 97–8
Hands, care of, 15
Hangovers, 21
Headaches, 21
Heart, weak, 21
Hoarseness, 22
Honey, 36
Hot-water bottle, 79

Ice cream stains, 58
Indigestion, 22

Influenza, 21
Ink, eradicator, 104
  invisible, 103-4
  stains, 58-9
Insomnia, 22
Iodine stains, 59
Iron, 48
Ironing, 70, 79
Itch, 22

Jam stains, 59
Jellyfish sting, 22

Kettle, fur in, 48-9
Kidney stones, 22
Knives, rust on, 49

Ladder, 49
Leaves, houseplant, 89
Lemon, 36
  stains, 59
Lettuce, 36
Lice, head, 21
  on pet birds, 95
Lilac, 89
Lilies, 89
Linen, waterproofing, 70
Linen cupboard, damp, 70
Linoleum, 80
Lipstick, removing from
  clothes, 59
Liqueur stains, 60
Liquorice stains, 60

Macaroni, 36
Marble, stains on, 63-4
Mayonnaise stains, 60
Meat, 36
Meatballs, 37
Medicine, taking, 22

Metal objects, 49
Mica, 49
Mice, 98
Milk, 37
  stains, 60
Mince, 37
Moles, 98
Mothproofing, 71
Moths, 98
Mud stains, 60
Mustard, 37

Nail polish stains, 60
Nails (metal), 80
Nausea, 22
Nerves, 23
Nettle rash, 22
Nettles, stinging, 90
Nicotine stains,
  on fingers, 14
  on material, 60
Nose, shiny, 16
  bleed, 23

Oats, 37
Oil lamps, 80
Oil stains, 60
Onions, 37-8
Oranges, 38
Oven, grease in, 49

Paint, 80-1
  stains, 60
Paintbrushes, 81
Pancakes, 38
Parcels, 104
Pastry, 38
Pâté, 38
Patent leather, 71
Peas, 38

Perfume stains, 61
Perspiration stains, 61
Piano, 104
Pigeons, 98
Pin cushion, 104
Pine, 89
Pineapple, 38
Ping-pong ball, 104
Plaster, ornaments, 50
    removing from clothes, 61
Pollen, 90
Poppies, 90
Porridge, spilt, 61
Potatoes, 38-9
Potting plants, 90
Pus stains, 61

Rabbits, 98
Rats, 98
Refrigerator smells, 50
Resin stains, 61
Rheumatism, 23
Rice, 39
Rope, strengthening, 81-2
Rust stains, 61

Salad oil, 40
Salt, 40
Salt-cellar, 82
Sausages, 40
Saw, 82
Scalp, 16
Scissors, 104
Scorch marks, 61-2
Screws, 82
Seasickness, 23
Sewing-machine needle, 104
Shampoo, as stain remover, 71
Shoe cleaning, 71-2
Shoelaces, 72

Shoe polish stains, 62
Silk ties, 72
Silver, 50, 104
Skin care, 16
Sleepwalking, 24
Snails, 98
Soap, 104-5
Soot stains, 62
Sore throat, 24
Soup, 40
Spectacles, 72
Sponge, 50
Stair carpet, 82
Stamps, 105
Steak, braising, 29
Steel, 50
Strawberries, 40
    stains, 62
String, 105
Suede, cleaning, 72
Sunburn, 24
Sunstroke, 24
Suntan, 16
    lotion, stains, 62
Sweat, 24
Sweater, 72-3
Sweet peas, 90

Tar stains, 62
Tea stains, 62-3
Teeth, cleaning, 16
Telephones, 105
Thermometer, 24
Thermos flask, 51
Ticks, 98-9
Tin opener, 51
Tin, stains on, 64
Tobacco, 105
Toenails, ingrowing, 25
Tomatoes, 40

Toothache, 25
Travel sickness, 25
Trousers, drying, 73
Tubes, 105
Tulips, 90

Umbrella, 73

Vase, 82
Velvet, 73
Verdigris, 51

Wallpaper, 51
  stains on, 64
Walnuts, 41
Warts, 25

Wash basin, stains in, 64
Washing, 73
Washing up, 51
Water-colours, 82
Watering houseplants, 91
Windows, 51–2, 82–3
Wine stains, 63
Wood, stains caused by, 63
  stains on, 64–5
Wooden posts, 83
Woodlice, 99
Woodworm, 99
Wool, 73

Yoghurt stains, 63

Zip fasteners, 73